Whales and Dolphins

Anita Ganeri

KINGFISHER

KINGFISHER

First published 2013 by Kingfisher
an imprint of Macmillan Children's Books
a division of Macmillan Publishers Limited
20 New Wharf Road, London N1 9RR
Basingstoke and Oxford
Associated companies throughout the world
www.panmacmillan.com

Illustrations by: Peter Bull Art Studio

ISBN 978-0-7534-3267-9

Copyright © Macmillan Children's Books 2013

1 3 5 7 9 8 6 4 2
1TR/0313/UTD/WKT/140MA

A CIP catalogue record for this book is available from
the British Library.

Printed in China

Picture credits

**The Publisher would like to thank the following
for permission to reproduce their material.**
(t = top, b = bottom, c = centre, l = left, r = right):
Pages 4–5 Frank Lane Picture Agency (FLPA)/Flip Nicklin/
Minden; 4br Naturepl/Jeff Rotman; 5cl Naturepl/Gabriel Rojo;
6 Getty/Paul Nicklin/NGS; 8tr Shutterstock/idreamphoto; 8b
Naturepl/Mark Carwardine; 9tr FLPA/Jean-Pierre Sylvestre/
Bios; 9cl Shutterstock/Tatiana Ivkovich; 9c Getty/OSF; 9br Getty/
Mark Carwardine; 10 Shutterstock/CampCrazy Photography;
12tl FLPA/Norbert Wu/Minden; 12cr Naturepl/David Tipling; 13tl
Getty/Brian J. Skerry/NGS; 13cr FLPA/Bios; 13bl AWL/Images/
Danita Delimont; 13br Seapics/Doug Perrine; 14 Alamy/Danita
Delimont; 16–17 FLPA/Flip Nicklin/Minden; 16cl FLPA/Flip Nicklin/
Minden; 16bl Alamy/WaterFrame; 16br FLPA/Flip Nicklin/Minden;
17tr Naturepl/Alex Mustard; 17br Naturepl/Brandon Cole; 18
FLPA/Newman; 20cl FLPA/Bios; 20b FLPA/Bios; 21tl FLPA/
Reinhard Dirschel; 21tr FLPA/Flip Nicklin/Minden; 21b Naturepl/
Todd Pusser; 22 Alamy/Kevin Schafer; 24tr Corbis/Isabel
Beasley/Reuters; 24b Corbis/Chor Sokunthea/Reuters; 25tr
Reuters/Andres Stapff; 25cl Reuters/Janghir Khan; 25cr Ardea/
Mark Carwardine; 25bl Seapics/Roland Seitre; 25br Corbis/
Christine Osborne; 26 SeaPics/Phillip Colla; 28cl Getty/Barcroft
Media; 28cr FLPA/Flip Nicklin/Minden; 28bl Corbis/Jeff Rotman;
28br Corbis/Tony Arruza; 29tr Getty/AFP Photo/Greg Wood;
29b Corbis/Ocean; 30tl Alamy/Steven J. Kazlowski; 30tr FLPA/
Flip Nicklin/Minden; 30ctl Nature/Sue Flood; 30ctr Nature/Mark
Carwardine; 30cbr Corbis/Michael Nicholson; 30bl Nature/Todd
Pusser; 31tr Nature/Mark Carwardine; 31cl Alamy/AF Archive;
31ctr FLPA/Frans Lanting; 31bl Specialist Stock/M. Lane/
WILDLIFE; 31br Shutterstock/idreamphoto.

More to explore

On some of the pages in this book, you will find coloured buttons with symbols on them. There are four different colours, and each belongs to a different topic. Choose a topic, follow its coloured buttons through the book, and you'll make some interesting discoveries of your own.

For example, on page 6 you'll find a green button, like this, next to a polar scene. The green buttons are about places where whales and dolphins live.

Page 27

Environment

There is a page number in the button. Turn to that page (page 27) to find a green button on another whale habitat. Follow all the steps through the book, and at the end of your journey you'll find out how the steps are linked, and discover even more information about this topic.

Record breakers

Whale stories   Communication

The other topics in this book are record breakers, whale stories and communication. Follow the steps and see what you can discover!

The whale family

Whales are mammals that live in the sea. The whale family also includes dolphins and porpoises. There are about 80 kinds. Like humans, they are warm-blooded and breathe air. They come to the surface to breathe.

Scientists study a blue whale from their boat

a bottlenose dolphin calf with its mother

Baby dolphins, whales and porpoises are looked after by their mothers and fed on milk. They stay with their mums for two to three years. A young whale is called a calf.

The blue whale is the biggest animal that has ever lived. It can grow up to 30m long and weigh as much as 35 elephants. The water helps to support its huge bulk.

sperm whale

blue whale

Whales are the largest members of the whale family. Some, such as blue, humpback and sperm whales, are called 'great whales' because of their size.

Whales look smooth, but like all mammals they have some hair.

whiskers around a right whale's mouth

vaquita porpoise

Porpoises are the smallest members of the whale family, about 2m long or less. They have blunter, rounder heads than dolphins, and no beaks.

Dolphins are 2m to 3m long. They have long, pointed snouts, called beaks. They are fast swimmers and are often very acrobatic.

white-beaked dolphin

Ocean home

Whales and dolphins live in oceans around the world, from warm, tropical waters to icy, polar seas. They swim, feed, breed and play in their ocean home. Some travel huge distances across the sea to feed and breed.

Page 27

What is this?

The Arctic Ocean is bitterly cold and partly covered in ice. Despite this, it is home to several kinds of whales. A group of belugas dive after their prey of fish. Nearby, a pod of narwhals cruises along. The males occasionally raise their long tusks above the water.

1 An adult beluga whale has white skin.

2 A beluga calf is grey but later turns white.

3 Thick blubber (fat) keeps this bowhead whale warm.

? This is a male narwhal's long tusk. It can grow up to 3m long.

3

4

5

6

Page 18

Page 26

4 Seabirds soar over the ocean, looking for fish.

5 A male narwhal has a long upper tooth called a tusk.

6 A female narwhal does not have a tusk.

Life in the sea

Whales and dolphins are perfectly adapted for life in the water. Their bodies are streamlined for swimming, with flippers for turning and balancing. They come to the surface to breathe air through small openings called blowholes.

dorsal (back) fin

This **dwarf minke whale** has a typical whale's body. Under its skin, it has a thick layer of fat called blubber. This helps to keep the whale warm in the sea.

blowhole

Minke whales live in seas around the world.

flipper

This **tail** belongs to a humpback whale. It has two parts, called flukes. Whales move their tails up and down to power their bodies through the water.

A right whale leaps out of the water. This is called breaching.

dorsal fin

The pointed **dorsal (back) fin** of an orca sticks up above the water. The fin can grow up to 1.8m high – as tall as an adult human.

finless porpoise

A single blowhole is found in toothed whales, such as sperm whales, orcas, dolphins and porpoises. As the animal breathes out, its 'blow' looks like a jet of steam.

sei whale

Double blowholes are found in baleen whales, such as fin, blue and sei whales. The two holes are side by side on the top of the head. Air goes in and out of the whale's body through its blowholes.

What is this?

Page 30

1 A spectacled porpoise is a fast swimmer.

2 A southern elephant seal sounds the alarm.

3 Dusky dolphins leap out of the water.

A group of sea lions and their pups are resting on a beach in South America. A pod of hungry orcas lurks offshore. Suddenly, one of the orcas races towards the sand and lunges at a pup. Seconds later, it grabs the unlucky pup in its jaws and heads back out to sea.

Hungry hunters

Whales and dolphins eat all kinds of sea animals. Toothed whales, such as orcas and dolphins, are active hunters. They chase fish and even seals and sea lions to eat. They have sharp teeth for grabbing prey, and can swim fast after their victims.

Page 15

Page 15

4

5

6

? This is a close-up of an orca's teeth. They are large and peg-like for grabbing prey.

Dolphins also use echolocation to find their way around.

Dolphins use **echolocation** to find their prey. They make clicking sounds that hit objects in the water and send back echoes. The dolphins listen for the echoes to work out where there are fish to eat.

Blue whales eat tonnes of tiny shrimps, called krill.

krill

Food and feeding

Toothed whales, such as orcas and dolphins, use their teeth for grabbing prey. Baleen whales, such as blue and humpback whales, have bristly brushes (baleen) inside their mouths instead of teeth. They use their baleen to sieve tiny creatures from the sea.

A dolphin's teeth are wide and cone-shaped for catching slippery prey, such as fish and squid. They are the same shape all along its jaw. A dolphin has between 60 and 100 teeth.

baleen

A baleen whale swims along with its mouth open. It gulps in water, then pushes it out again through its baleen. The baleen works like a sieve, trapping any food.

pointed teeth

humpback whales feeding

Bubble 'nets' are used by humpback whales to trap food. The whales blow bubbles around a shoal of fish or krill. Then they swim up through the middle with their mouths wide open.

This Bryde's whale has a pleated throat that expands when it feeds.

sardines

1 A sperm whale breaches (leaps out of the water).

2 A female sperm whale is giving birth.

3 The calf is born tail first.

What is this?

Page 10

Birth of a whale

A baby whale, or calf, is born underwater, usually tail first. Its mother nudges it gently towards the surface so that it can take its first breath. The calf is able to swim straight away. Most whales have one calf at a time – twins are very rare.

4

5

6

Page 29

Page 30

It is breeding time for these sperm whales. A group of females and their young swims through the ocean. Some of the females are mothers with calves. Others are 'aunties' who help to look after the calves while their mothers go to find food. A whale calf stays with its mum for two to three years, feeding on her milk.

This is a sperm whale's wrinkly skin.

Family life

Many whales and dolphins live in family groups, called pods or schools. There may be tens or even hundreds of animals in a group. They help each other to find food and care for young. They have special ways of talking to each other underwater.

Male narwhals use their long tusks for jousting during the breeding season. They fight to win over females and to establish their position in the pod.

Male humpback whales hang in the water and sing songs to attract females. Each song can last for about half an hour and the male may sing it over and over again.

A fin whale has the loudest voice of any whale or dolphin.

Atlantic spotted dolphins live in close, strongly bonded pods, made up of males, females and young. The pod members feed and swim together, staying close if there is danger nearby.

Older animals are covered in light and dark spots.

A bottlenose whale mother swims with her calf. Young bottlenose whales are usually much darker in colour than their parents.

Belugas are nicknamed 'sea canaries' because they whistle and chirp like birds. They also click and squeak. They use these sounds to communicate with other members of the pod.

A long journey

Each year, many whales make long journeys across the sea to find the best places to feed and breed. This is called migration. The whales swim in groups, occasionally spy-hopping – lifting their heads above water to look around.

Page 11

What are these?

1. A grey whale dives for food.

2. Anchovies are the whales' prey.

3. Hungry orcas lurk nearby.

? These are barnacles (a kind of shellfish) on a grey whale's back.

3

4

Page 30

A group of grey whales is nearing the end of its migration. The whales have swum from their feeding grounds in the Arctic Ocean to their breeding grounds off the coast of Mexico – a distance of around 10,000km. A pod of orcas looks on, ready to prey on the weak or sick.

5

6

Page 30

4 A grey whale spy-hops to look around.

5 The leatherback turtle is the largest sea turtle.

6 A manta ray has wing-like fins.

On the move

A whale or dolphin's body is streamlined for swimming. The animal powers through the water in smooth, arching movements, thanks to its muscular tail. As the tail moves up and down, it propels the whale's body forwards.

Whales rest by 'logging' – hanging still in the water.

a humpback whale logging

A Dall's porpoise does everything at high speed, even surfacing to breathe. In rough seas, a spray of water appears from its head and along its back. This is known as a rooster tail.

A sperm whale regularly dives to depths of up to 3,000m to find food. A typical dive lasts about 45 minutes but a whale can hold its breath for more than 2 hours.

Sperm whales dive almost vertically (straight down).

a Dall's porpoise with a 'rooster tail' of spray

Spinner dolphins are amazing acrobats. They make spectacular leaps high into the air, twisting and spinning as they jump. They can spin seven times in a single leap.

a spinner dolphin in mid-leap

Dolphins are speedy swimmers. As they swim, they often make long, low leaps out of the water, almost as if they are bouncing along. This is called 'porpoising'.

a trio of dolphins porpoising at high speed

In the river

Several kinds of dolphins live in rivers and lakes. They are specially adapted to their homes. Most are almost blind, since eyes are no use in the murky water. Instead, like their seagoing cousins, the dolphins use echolocation (see page 12) to find their way.

What is this?

1. A tucuxi spy-hops above the surface.

2. A boto looks for food in the murky water.

3. Piranhas also live in the Amazon river.

? This is a boto's long beak. It is full of small, pointed teeth for catching fish.

Page 19

5

6

4

It is early evening on a muddy stretch of the Amazon river in South America. A group of botos has come out to feed. These long-beaked river dolphins share their home with giant otters, piranha fish and tucuxis – another kind of dolphin.

4 A boto rests on its side, flipper in the air.

5 Sleek giant otters hunt fish in the river.

6 Botos have a bulging forehead or 'melon'.

River dolphins

Most river dolphins are very rare. They face many risks in the wild. They may become trapped in fishing nets or be injured by boats' propellers. Their main threat, though, is pollution. Some river dolphins are also hunted by people for food.

The Irrawaddy dolphin is found in rivers in southeast Asia, where it can swim more than 1,000km upstream. It also lives in shallow, sheltered coastal waters.

The snubfin dolphin lives off the northern coast of Australia. It was named as a new species in 2005. Before this, scientists thought that it was a kind of Irrawaddy dolphin.

an Irrawaddy dolphin peeking above the surface

This baby **La Plata dolphin** was lucky to be rescued. It had become tangled in a fishing net. Many dolphins die in this way because they cannot reach the surface to breathe.

The Yangtze river dolphin was declared extinct in 2006. It was only found in the Yangtze river, China, one of the busiest and dirtiest rivers in the world.

▲ Ganges river dolphin sticks its head out of the water.

Females have longer beaks than males.

Dams built across rivers cause problems for dolphins. They block the flow of the river and the dolphins cannot travel to find food or mates.

This **Indus river dolphin** was rescued from an irrigation canal (built to carry river water to farmers' fields). Stuck there, it would not have been able to find food to eat.

Page 14

① Two harbour seals swim towards the boat.

② A pair of minke whales swims offshore.

③ A right whale breaches with a splash.

What is this?

Off the coast of Boston, USA, these whale watchers are in for a treat. A school of dolphins swims alongside their boat while, right ahead, a humpback whale is breaching – a spectacular sight. In the distance are minke and right whales. An onboard scientist makes an undersea recording of the whales' calls.

Watching whales

The more we find out about whales by studying them in the wild, the better we can protect them. Watching whales can be thrilling, whether it's from the air, the shore or from boats. Just be patient and keep your distance so that you don't disturb the whales!

4 Another whale-watching boat stops nearby.

5 White-sided dolphins leap above the waves.

6 A scientist prepares to throw recording equipment into the sea.

27

Page 23

↻ These are scars on a humpback whale's body made by a boat propeller.

Saving whales

Around the world, whales and dolphins face many threats. They are hunted, caught in fishing nets, and harmed by litter and pollution in the sea. Scientists and conservationists work hard to study these amazing animals and to protect them.

Filming whales is one way to study them in their natural habitat. Scientists can identify particular whales and follow them as they go about their daily lives.

This satellite transmitter is fixed to a beluga whale.

The transmitter sends signals to a satellite.

In some places, people can swim with dolphins.

Whaling means hunting whales for their meat and other products. This old carving shows a whaling ship. Today, most whaling is banned.

Saving whales that are stranded is a difficult task. Here, volunteers in Australia pour water over beached false killer whales to keep them wet and cool until they can be re-floated.

Whales can become stranded if they hunt too close to shore.

Fishing nets can be deadly to whales and dolphins. If they get trapped in one, they cannot come to the surface to breathe and may drown. About 1,000 die in this way every day.

Record breakers

Bowhead whales have the longest baleen plates of any whale. They can be more than 4m long. When the whale's mouth is closed, its big bottom jaw covers the baleen.

baleen

Grey whales make the longest migration of any whale, or any mammal. Their yearly journey from Mexico to the Arctic and back again is a round trip of around 20,000km.

Environment

The beluga is superbly adapted to its **Arctic Ocean** home. It is able to locate the rare air spaces under the ice, and its white skin helps to camouflage it.

Watching whales in their **natural habitat** is growing more popular. But it is vital that any money made is used to help protect the whales and their environment.

whale spy-hopping

Whale stories

narwhal's tusk

The legendary **unicorn's** spiral horn is based on the narwhal's tusk. In reality, there is nothing magical about the tusk – it is just a very long top tooth.

The Bible tells the tale of **Jonah,** who is saved from drowning when a whale swallows him. Jonah spends three days and nights in the whale.

Communication

Orcas use **whistles, clicks** and other sounds to keep in touch with the other members of their pod while they are swimming or hunting. Each pod has its own set of sounds.

Sperm whales use **patterns of clicks** to communicate. Each whale has a different pattern. Baby whales have to learn how to 'speak', just as human babies do.

More to explore

Orcas are the fastest-swimming whales. They can reach a top speed of 55km/h – about six times faster than the quickest human swimmer.

orcas speeding along the surface

Sperm whales have the largest heads of any animal, and the largest brains. A sperm whale brain weighs nearly 8kg – that's five times as much as a human's brain.

The tucuxi is at home in **salt and freshwater** habitats. It lives in the Amazon river and around the edges of the southern Atlantic. It feeds on catfish, small crabs and shrimps.

Grey whales breed in warm, sheltered **bays and lagoons** along the coast of Mexico. The shallow water helps to protect the babies from shark attacks.

grey whale calf

white sperm whale

Moby Dick is a story about a whaling ship trying to track down a ferocious white sperm whale. The book was based on sightings of an actual whale in the early 1800s.

The **Haida people** of North America believe that orcas are the most powerful animals in the sea. They tell of orcas that live in amazing underwater cities.

Haida carving

Echolocation allows dolphins to build up a sound picture of their surroundings. In murky river water, this ability is much more useful than having good eyesight.

boto river dolphin

Breaching is when a whale or dolphin launches itself into the air, then falls back into the water with a great big splash. This may be a way of sending signals, or it may simply be for fun.

Index